📖 DORLING KINDERSLEY *READERS*

Level 1

A Day at Greenhill Farm
Truck Trouble
Tale of a Tadpole
Surprise Puppy!
Duckling Days
A Day at Seagull Beach
Whatever the Weather
Busy Buzzy Bee
Big Machines
Wild Baby Animals
A Bed for the Winter
Born to be a Butterfly

Dinosaur's Day
Feeding Time
Diving Dolphin
Rockets and Spaceships
LEGO: Trouble at the Bridge
LEGO: Secret at Dolphin Bay
JPD: A Day in the Life of a Builder
JPD: A Day in the Life of a Dancer
JPD: A Day in the Life of
   a Firefighter
JPD: A Day in the Life of
   a Teacher

Level 2

Dinosaur Dinners
Fire Fighter!
Bugs! Bugs! Bugs!
Slinky, Scaly Snakes!
Animal Hospital
The Little Ballerina
Munching, Crunching, Sniffing
   and Snooping
The Secret Life of Trees
Winking, Blinking, Wiggling
   and Waggling

Astronaut: Living in Space
Twisters!
Holiday! Celebration Days
   around the World
The Story of Pocahontas
Horse Show
Survivors: The Night the
   Titanic Sank
Eruption! The Story of Volcanoes
LEGO: Castle Under Attack!
LEGO: Rocket Rescue

Level 3

Spacebusters
Beastly Tales
Shark Attack!
Titanic
Invaders from Outer Space
Movie Magic
Plants Bite Back!
Time Traveler
Bermuda Triangle
Tiger Tales
Aladdin
Heidi
Zeppelin: The Age of the Airship

Spies
Terror on the Amazon
Disasters at Sea
The Story of Anne Frank
Abraham Lincoln: Lawyer,
   Leader, Legend
George Washington: Soldier,
   Hero, President
LEGO: Mission to the Arctic
NFL: Troy Aikman
NFL: Super Bowl Heroes
MLB: Home Run Heroes
MLB: Roberto Clemente

A Note to Parents

Dorling Kindersley Readers is a compelling program for beginning readers, designed in conjunction with leading literacy experts, including Dr. Linda Gambrell, Director of the School of Education at Clemson University. Dr. Gambrell has served on the Board of Directors of the International Reading Association and as President of the National Reading Conference.

Beautiful illustrations and superb full-color photographs combine with engaging, easy-to-read stories to offer a fresh approach to each subject in the series. Each *Dorling Kindersley Reader* is guaranteed to capture a child's interest while developing his or her reading skills, general knowledge, and love of reading.

The four levels of *Dorling Kindersley Readers* are aimed at different reading abilities, enabling you to choose the books that are exactly right for your child:

Level 1 – Beginning to read
Level 2 – Beginning to read alone
Level 3 – Reading alone
Level 4 – Proficient readers

The "normal" age at which a child begins to read can be anywhere from three to eight years old, so these levels are intended only a general guideline.

No matter which level you select, you can be sure that you are helping your child learn to read, then read to learn!

Dorling [DK] Kindersley

LONDON, NEW YORK, SYDNEY, DELHI, PARIS,
MUNICH, and JOHANNESBURG

Project Editor Caryn Jenner
Art Editor Jane Horne
Senior Art Editor Clare Shedden
Series Editor Deborah Lock
US Editor Adrienne Betz
Production Shivani Pandey
Picture Researcher Angela Anderson
Jacket Designer Karen Burgess

Space Consultant
Carole Stott

Reading Consultant
Linda Gambrell, Ph.D.

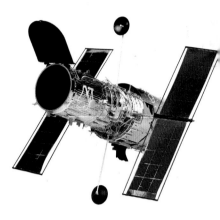

First American Edition, 2001
00 01 02 03 04 05 10 9 8 7 6 5 4 3 2 1
Published in the United States by DK Publishing, Inc.
95 Madison Avenue, New York, New York 10016

Library of Congress Cataloging-in-Publication Data
Wallace, Karen.
    Rockets and spaceships / by Karen Wallace. – 1st American ed.
    p. cm – (Dorling Kindersley readers)
    ISBN 0-7894-7360-7 (hardcover) – ISBN 0-7894-7359-3 (pbk.)
    1. Space Vehicles–Juvenile literature. [1. Space vehicles.]
    I. Title. II. Series.

TL793 .W325 2001
629.47–dc21   00-056974

Color reproduction by Colourscan, Singapore
Printed and bound in China by L Rex Printing Co., Ltd.

The publisher would like to thank the following for their
kind permission to reproduce their images:
Position key: c=center; b=bottom; l=left; r=right; t=top

European Space Agency: 19t, 20t, 29c; N.A.S.A.
24-25 background. **Eurospace Centre, Transinne, Belgium:** 6-7.
London Planetarium: 6. **N.A.S.A.:** front jacket, 4, 5, 8, 9tr, 9b,
10-11, 12-13, 14, 15, 16-17, 18, 26tl, 28-29, 31. **Planet Earth
Pictures:** 22-23, 22b. **Space and Rocket Center,
Alabama:** 24-25 foreground. **Science Photo Library:** 26-27.
N.A.S.A. Kennedy Space Center: front jacket, back jacket.
Paul Weston: illustration 30cl.

see our complete
catalog at

www.dk.com

DK DORLING KINDERSLEY *READERS*

BEGINNING **1** TO READ

Rockets and Spaceships

Written by Karen Wallace

DK

A Dorling Kindersley Book

5... 4... 3... 2... 1...
Blast Off!

Rumble... rumble...
ROOAAARRRR!
A rocket takes off
into the sky.
It zooms up and
away from Earth.

rocket

The rocket flies very far,
VERY FAST.

Rumble
Rumble ROOAAARRR!

Rockets help us to
explore space.
Astronauts are scientists
who travel in space.

astronaut

They travel in a spaceship
at the top of a rocket.

The rocket takes
the spaceship up to space.
Then the rocket falls away.

Astronauts can see
the Moon and stars
in space.

planet

They can see
planets, too.
Our planet is called Earth.
This is how astronauts see Earth
from space.

Some astronauts have traveled
to the Moon.
They explored the Moon
and did experiments.

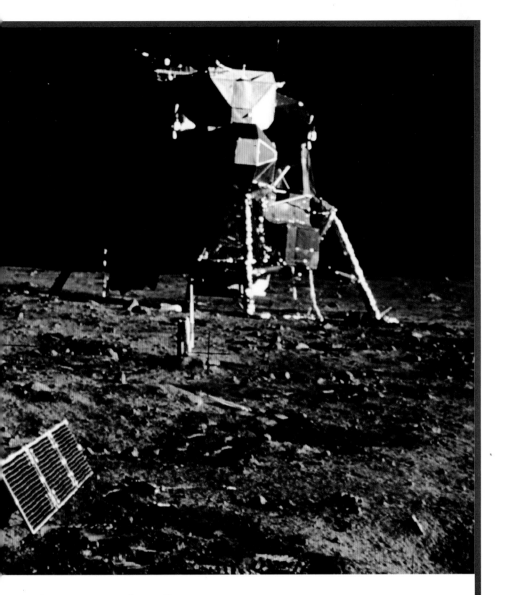

They picked up
dust and rocks
for scientists to study
back on Earth.

Sometimes, astronauts
"walk" in space.
Walking in space is not
like walking on Earth.

Astronauts must use a special rope which keeps them attached to their spaceship. Otherwise, they would float away!

This is a space shuttle.
It is part rocket, part plane.
Astronauts have used it
for many trips to space.
The plane part of the space shuttle
can be used again and again.
It takes off like a rocket,
then it glides back to Earth
and lands like an airplane.

rocket
engine

The space shuttle uses
rocket engines to blast off.
When the rocket engines fall away
the shuttle plane flies into space.

A space shuttle does
many different jobs.
It can carry satellites
as well as astronauts.

satellite

Different kinds of satellites
do different jobs from space.
Special computers
help the satellites keep
their correct position
above the Earth.

The satellites send
and receive signals
which help us every day.

Some satellites send signals from one part of the world to another.

We use these signals when we watch television or talk on the telephone.

Other satellites take pictures of the weather from high above Earth.

This picture shows a storm coming!

The Hubble
Space Telescope
is a very
special satellite.

It is a telescope
and a camera,
which can see
stars and planets
that are millions
of miles away.

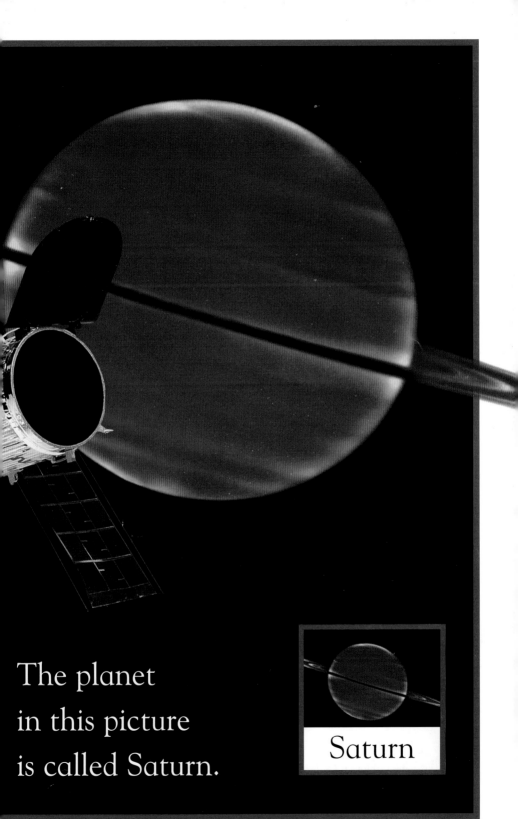

The planet
in this picture
is called Saturn.

Saturn

Probes are machines
that explore space
on their own.
They do not carry
astronauts.

probe

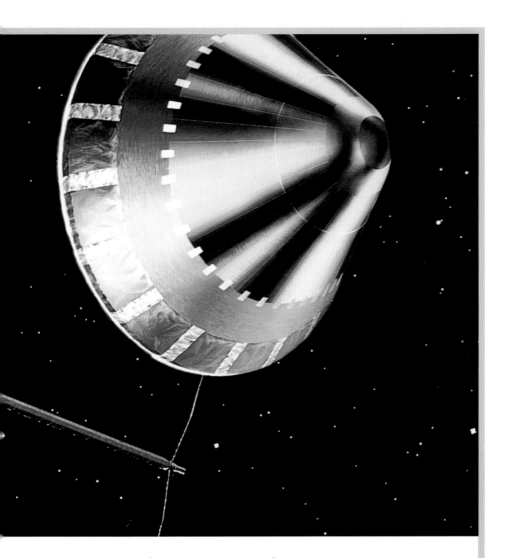

Space probes visit planets
that are very far away.
They take pictures
and send them back
to scientists on Earth.

Mars

A space probe carried
this tiny rover
to a planet called Mars.
The rover explored Mars
and studied the rocks.

Some people think
there might be
life on Mars.
One day, scientists
will know for sure!

Some astronauts
stay in space
for months
and months.

The space station
becomes their home.
They do experiments
and learn about
living in space.

Imagine eating
and sleeping
in a place
where everything floats!

There are still so many secrets
to discover.
Scientists invent new rockets
and spaceships all the time.
There are even plans
to build a space hotel.

Greetings from **space**

Who knows?
One day **you** might go
on vacation in space!

Picture word list

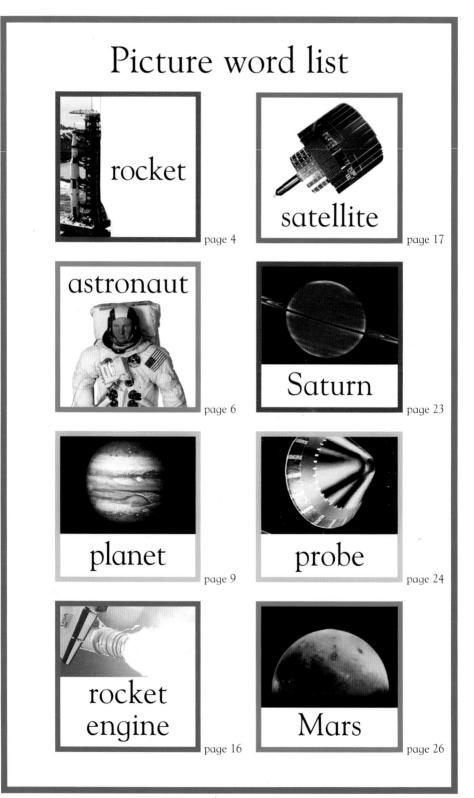

rocket

page 4

satellite

page 17

astronaut

page 6

Saturn

page 23

planet

page 9

probe

page 24

rocket engine

page 16

Mars

page 26